SHE STARTED IT!

A *BABY BLUES* Cartoon Collection

Rick Kirkman and Jerry Scott
Foreword by Lynn Johnston

CB
CONTEMPORARY
BOOKS
A TRIBUNE NEW MEDIA COMPANY

Library of Congress Cataloging-in-Publication Data

Kirkman, Rick.
  [Baby blues.   Selections]
  She started it! : a Baby Blues cartoon
collection / Rick Kirkman and Jerry Scott :
foreword by Lynn Johnston.
      p.   cm.
  ISBN 0-8092-3266-9 (alk. paper)
  I. Scott, Jerry, 1955–   .   II. Title.
PN6728.B25K57   1995
741.5'973—dc20   95-30787
                                  CIP

Published by Contemporary Books, Inc.
Two Prudential Plaza, Chicago, Illinois 60601-6790
Manufactured in the United States of America
International Standard Book Number: 0-8092-3266-9
10   9   8   7   6   5   4   3   2   1

To Sukey, always.
                    R.K.

To Mom and Pop with love.
                    J.S.

Foreword

When it was announced two years ago that a new "family" comic strip was about to be launched, a well-acquainted rabble of cartoonists waited with anxious curiosity to see what the blessed union of Jerry Scott and Rick Kirkman would produce. Having known them both for some time (and having seen them in action on a number of memorable partying occasions), we knew they were capable of just about anything . . . which is now evident from the howling success of "Baby Blues."

From their mutual pens has emerged one of the truest and funniest accounts of raising a baby ever to grace the comics page. It's also a kind and contemporary glimpse into the lives of a nurturing couple who, once bent on "doing everything right," are now merely bent—and doing the best they can.

Naturally, we cartoonists welcomed this new comic strip with open admiration. ("Damn. They're good.") No two families are alike, however, even in the comics. Although we cover some of the same territory and discuss similar subjects, we do so from varied and differing points of view, dredging up scenes from our pasts and often revealing more about ourselves in our work than we sometimes care to. (I worry about these guys.) More friends than rivals, we are part of an ever-widening self-help group whose motto goes beyond "a picture is worth a thousand words." We get to write the words as well. This is therapy, and we're willing to share it all.

Having said this, it is my great pleasure to introduce the second published collection of wonderful whinings and witticisms from the creators of "Baby Blues."

Put the kids to bed,
put your feet up,
and, knowing that you're
not alone . . . read on!

Lynn Johnston
Creator, "For Better or for Worse"

7

9

BABY BLUES®

RICK KIRKMAN / JERRY SCOTT BY

12

13

15

16

19

22

24

25

27

30

BABY BLUES

RICK KIRKMAN / JERRY SCOTT

40

41

44

45

48

52

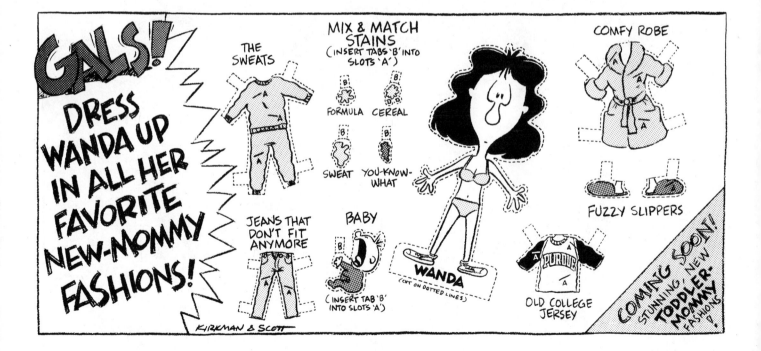

54

58

BABY BLUES

BY RICK KIRKMAN / JERRY SCOTT

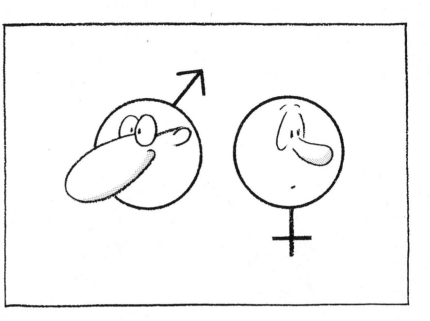

KIRKMAN & SCOTT

64

66

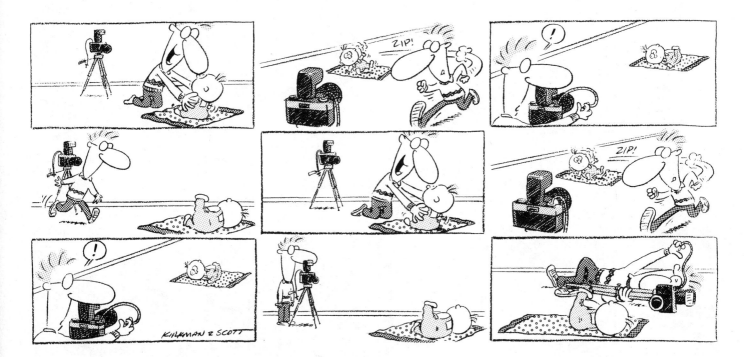

70

72

73

74

79

BABY BLUES®

BY RICK KIRKMAN / JERRY SCOTT

CHILD THING
(SUNG TO THE TUNE OF THE TROGGS' "WILD THING")

WAAAA! CHILD THING!
YOU MAKE MY EARS RING!
YOU MAKE EVERYTHING—
DROOLEY!
CHILD THING!

(GUITAR) DAH-DER-DA-DERRR
CHILD THING, I KNOW YOU'RE TEETHING...
DAH-DER-DA-DERRR
AND I HOPE I CAN ENDURE!
DAH-DER-DA-DERRR
SO COME ON... SLEEP TONIGHT...
DAH-DER-DA-DERRR
I BEG YOU.

CHILD THING!
I KNOW YOUR GUMS STING.
I'VE GOT TEETHING RINGS—
COOOLIN'.
CHILD THING!

DAH-DER-DA-DERRR
CHILD THING, YOU NEED SOME NUMZIT...
DAH-DER-DA-DERRR
OR MAYBE YOUR ANBESOL!
DAH-DER-DA-DERRR
SO COME ON... SLEEP TONIGHT...
DA-DER-DA-DERRR
YOU OWE ME.

CHILD THING!
YOU TUG MY HEART STRINGS.
ISN'T ANYTHING—
SOOOTHING?
CHILD THING!

COME ON, COME ON
CHILD THING...
HUSH UP, HUSH UP
CHILD THING...
TICKLE! TICKLE!
CHILD THING....

(WITH APOLOGIES TO THE TROGGS)
KIRKMAN & SCOTT

81

84

85

87

91

93

97

98

105

109

111

114

117

BABY BLUES®

BY RICK KIRKMAN / JERRY SCOTT

123

124

THE END

Celebrate the birth of a family.

BABY BLUES

This is going to be tougher than we thought.

By Rick Kirkman & Jerry Scott
Foreword by Cathy Guisewite